The Mountain Mea
Josiah Gi

MW01028521

i

NOTE TO SECOND AND FUTURE EDITIONS

Because of the faulty memory of an aged Mormon, who gave me the name of Isaac Laney as that of the man who was brutally beaten at Parowan, in southwestern Utah, because he sold a few onions to the emigrants who perished at the Mountain Meadows, a slight error crept into the first edition of "The Mountain Meadows Massacre."

Since its publication I have been most fortunate in meeting a wealthy man, now residing at Oakland, California, who lived next door to William Laney at Parowan at the time of the massacre, and from him learned the truth of the incident. His recollection of that incident has been verified by reference to a letter received a year ago from Judge James S. Aden of Tennessee, whose brother was a victim of the religion-crazed fanatics who exterminated Captain Charles Fancher's companions at the Mountain Meadows. Judge Aden's recollection of Laney's name was DeLaney. And because of the fact that I could learn nothing of any man by that name the Judge's interesting story of how his father aided William Laney, while the latter was a Mormon missionary, and how his brother was entertained by William Laney at Parowan, and given a few onions, was omitted from the first edition. It is now given in full. Also, at the recent Mormon general conference, I met the nephew of William Laney, and who told me that it was his uncle instead of his father, Isaac Laney, who lived at Parowan.

The above explanation has been given for purpose of disarming Mormon critics who are ever alert to even the slightest discrepancies that may find their way into the writings of those who presume to criticise the conduct and motives of the Mormon leaders.

JOSIAH F. GIBBS.

Salt Lake City, Utah, October 17th, 1910.

INTRODUCTION.

Some five years ago a prominent Salt Lake editor, in a letter to the writer, said: "The Mountain Meadows massacre is an incident that should be forgotten." The gentleman, a well-known Gentile, was in error, the human family learns only by experience. The lessons taught by the tragedies of the past come down to us in the form of history and become danger signals along the highway of advancing civilization, and warn us of the peril that marches hand in hand with human passions, with ignorance and superstition.

Speaking specifically, the Mountain Meadows massacre should not be forgotten as long as Mormon writers, pulpiteers and missionaries use the "Missouri Persecutions," the "Martyrdom of Joseph and Hyrum Smith," and the "Expulsion of the Saints from Nauvoo" as influences for proselyting. Nor should the discussion of any prominent tragedy cease until the causes that unerringly led up to the act shall have been eradicated, or until the lesson that it teaches is no longer necessary. The Mountain Meadows massacre should be kept before the public until unquestioning obedience to the will of the Mormon "prophets" shall be no longer exacted from the Mormon people, or until its deadening, damning influence is exterminated. Those who suggest such lapses of memory as that suggested by the Salt Lake editor do so in the interest of "peace in Utah," a "peace" that would be purchased by the surrender of justice to injustice, of right to wrong, of the present to the future—a surrender in Utah of moral progress and civil liberty to mercenary advantages and political bribes held out by the "prophets" and the Mormon and pro-Mormon press as the price of silence.

AGENCIES OF WHICH THE MASSACRE WAS THE LOGICAL RESULT.

The details of the Mountain Meadows massacre have been repeatedly told. Embittered Mormon "apostates" and greedy romancers have distorted the awful incidents; Mormon historians and subsidized writers have submerged the truth and endeavored to shift the burthen of the terrible crime to the Indians; and thus far none of them have, seemingly, been able to grasp the elusive forces that unerringly led up to the tragedy, or they have failed to state them.

With malice toward none, least of all toward the misguided assassins, and in a spirit of even-handed justice, the attempt will be made to assemble the fragments of causation and history and join them together in a consecutive narrative.

And it is well to here remark that the story of the massacre is largely drawn from the evidence of unwilling Mormon witnesses who testified during the second trial of John D. Lee; from close personal contact with the religious and social life of Utah from 1857 to the present time; from an intimate acquaintance with the people of southern Utah, and from a personal study of the locality known as the Mountain Meadows.

An intelligible grasp of the remarkable religious and social conditions that existed in Utah just prior to the massacre, and of which it was one of the logical results, cannot be imparted without quoting from the sermons of some of the Mormon "prophets." And it is a fact well known to Mormon leaders and historians that the expulsion of the Latter-day Saints from Missouri, the killing of Joseph and Hyrum Smith, and the expulsion of the church from Illinois were but the logical results of the "revelations," sermons and writings of the Mormon leaders, and which inspired the rank and file of the Mormons with grotesquely exaggerated views of the religious and political mission of Mormonism, and of their own importance.

Following are excerpta from a few of the "prophets' "sermons:

"God made Aaron to be the mouthpiece of the children of Israel, and he will make me to be God to you in his stead, and the elders to be mouth for me; and if you don't like it you must lump it."—From sermon by the "Prophet" Joseph Smith, Jr., Nauvoo, April, 1844; clipped from the Mormon Deseret News of July 15, 1857.

"The first principle of our cause and work is to understand that there is a prophet in the church, and that he is at the head of the Church of Christ on earth. Who called Joseph Smith to be a prophet? Did the people or God? God, and not the people, called him. Had the people gathered together and appointed one of their number to be a prophet, he would have been accountable to the people, but, inasmuch as he was called of God, and not by the people, he is accountable to God only . . . . and not to any man on earth. The twelve apostles are accountable to the prophet and not to the church for the course they pursue, and we have learned to go and do, as the prophet tells us."—From sermon by Brigham Young, at Nauvoo, 1843, published in Millennial Star, Liverpool, England, Vol. XXI., page 741.

"The fact of the matter is, when a man says 'you can direct me spiritually, but not temporally,' he lies in the presence of God; that is, if he has got intelligence enough to know what he is talking about."— From sermon by Joseph F. Smith (the present-day Mormon "prophet") at Provo, Utah; from the Deseret News, May 20, 1896.

The above quotations prove beyond the possibility of successful contradiction that the "prophets" of the Mormon church are, if their claims be accepted, vicegerents of God, that they act "in his stead"; that those of the Mormon people who deny the right of the "prophets" to "direct" them "temporally," "lie in the presence of God," and that the "prophets" are "accountable to God only, and not to any man on earth."

Also from President Brigham Young we learn that "we (the Mormons) have learned to go and do as the prophet tells us."

The subserviency of even the apostles of the Mormon church is well illustrated in the following:

"Now, whatever I might have obtained in the shape of learning, by searching and study respecting the arts and sciences of men—whatever principles I may have imbibed during my scientific researches, yet, if the prophet of God should tell me that a certain principle or theory which I might have learned was not true, I do not care what my ideas might have been, I should consider it my duty, at the suggestion of my file leader, to abandon that principle or theory."—From sermon by Apostle Wilford Woodruff at Salt Lake City, April 9, 1857, recorded in Journal of Discourses, Vol. I., page 83.

And in the face of the plain assertions of their leaders the Mormon people deny that they are ruled spiritually and temporally by one man—that they are slaves to the dicta of one man who claims to rule them by the authority and in the name and stead of God! But when the dupes of the Mormon "prophets" deny that self-evident fact they should remember that they "lie in the presence of God."

DOCTRINE OF "BLOOD ATONEMENT" AND ITS RESULTS.

Necessarily, the believer in unquestioning obedience to the dictum of one man, or his agent or agents, is a fanatic, and there is not a devout Mormon on earth who would not commit murder if he were ordered to do so by the chief "prophet" or one of his agents in whom he had confidence. If he would not obey the order then he is not a "firm believer in the (Mormon) faith." The voice of the "prophet" is the voice of God to him, and he has no alternative but to "go and do as he is told." Otherwise, "he lies in the presence of God."

And the reader will readily comprehend the awful significance of the combination of blind obedience and the doctrine of blood atonement, or the doctrine that one must submit to capital punishment for certain offenses which, as the Mormon "prophets" claim, were not included in the atonement of the Son of God. Add to that combination the fact that those blood atonement executions are to be carried out under the authority of the leader of a religious organization, and not under any civil process, and one will have a partial perception of the conditions that existed in Utah under the rule of the "prophets" from their occupation of Utah, in 1847, to 1880. Mormons deny the existence of those conditions, but they will not deny the accuracy of the following quotations:

"There is not a man or woman who violates the covenants made with their God (in the Mormon temples), that will not be required to pay the debt. The blood of Christ will never wipe that out, your own blood must atone for it; and the judgments of the Almighty will come, sooner or later, and every man or woman will have to atone for breaking their covenants."—From sermon by Brigham Young, March 16, 1856, Journal of Discourses, Vol. III., page 247.

"What do you suppose they would say in old Massachusetts should they hear that the Latter-day Saints had received a revelation or commandment to 'lay judgment to the line and righteousness to the plummet'? What would they say in old Connecticut? They would raise a universal howl of 'how wicked the Mormons are. They are killing the evildoers who are among them. Why, I hear that they kill the wicked away up yonder in Utah.' . . . What do I care for the wrath of man? No more than I do for the chickens that run in my dooryard. I am here to teach the ways of the Lord, and lead men to life everlasting; but if they have not a mind to go there, I wish them to keep out of my path."—From sermon by Brigham Young in 1855, Journal of Discourses, Vol. III., page 50.

"If any miserable scoundrels come here, cut their throats." From red hot blood atonement sermon by Brigham Young, Journal of Discourses, Vol. II., page 311. At the conclusion of the injunction to "cut their throats," "all the people said 'amen!' "

"I would ask how many covenant breakers there are in this city and in this kingdom (the Mormon 'kingdom of God')? I believe that there are a great many; and if they are covenant breakers, we need a place designated where we can shed their blood. . . . If any of you ask, do I mean you, I answer yes. If any woman asks, do I mean her, I answer yes. . . . We have been trying long enough with these people, and I go in for letting the sword of the Almighty be unsheathed, not only in word but in deed."—From sermon by Jedediah M. Grant, second counselor to Brigham Young, Journal of Discourses, Vol. IV., pp. 49-50.

It is not necessary to give the details of the blood atonement murder of William R. Parrish and his son Beason for "apostasy," at Springville, in 1856; of the murder of Rosmos Anderson by the leading priesthood of the Parowan "stake of Zion" in 1856, because Philip Klingensmith, bishop of Cedar City, Utah, coveted the buxom Scandinavian stepdaughter of Anderson as his plural wife, and whom Anderson also wanted as his plural, and with whom, as alleged, he had committed adultery as the last and surest effort to secure a "recommend" to enter the "holy order of celestial marriage"; of the castration of Tom Lewis, at Manti, Utah, in 1856, because Bishop Warren Snow was lecherously ambitious to polygamously marry the girl with whom Lewis was keeping company; of the inexpressibly cowardly murder of William Hatton at Fillmore, 1856, by a man who could be named, and who was the agent of the "prophets, seers and revelators" at Salt Lake City, and whose handsome widow the unspeakable "Prophet" Heber C. Kimball soon after added to his celestial harem; of the murder, by prophetic instructions, at Farmington, during the spring of 1858, of four of the Aiken party, and while "Johnston's" army at Ham's Fork was preparing to enter Utah, and of the cowardly assassination of two others of the Aiken party by a present high churchman and his companion, who, under pretense of conducting them from Utah by the southern route to California, shot them in the back at a point some four or five miles south of Nephi, about 110 miles south of Salt Lake City; of the midnight murder, later on, of King, Brassfield and others who became obnoxious to the Mormon leaders. This is an abbreviated history of the Mountain Meadows massacre—not of the entire diabolical results of the teaching of unquestioning obedience and blood atonement by the vicegerents of the Mormon god.

Any one with ordinary intelligence can comprehend the terrible results of the license to murder which is embraced in the excerpta that have been quoted from the bloodthirsty sermons of two of the chief "prophets" of the Mormon church.

The preaching of blood atonement was accompanied by two years— 1856-1857—of hysterical repentance called the Mormon "reformation." The larger portion of the "Saints" confessed their sins to the "block teachers," to the "ward bishops," or, as in many instances, to Brigham Young, to whom many of the sinful Saints went with their tales of iniquity. It was a time of confession, of the "renewal of covenants" by rebaptism, and the intensification of indescribable fanaticism, frenzy and violence.

The reason for those violent outbreaks on the part of the prophets is alleged to have been the effect of the unrestrained liberty, even license, of frontier life, which affects alike the saint and the sinner; the latter, of course, being the more willing victim. Even some of the "saints of the Most High" descended to stealing and worse crimes. That, and the influx of traders, trappers and others not of the Mormon faith, created apprehension on the part of the "prophets" that the "kingdom of God," which they had "established in the top of the mountains," would perish because of the iniquity of the people.

It was the hope that it might check the carnival of crime that prompted the Mormon leaders to inaugurate the "reformation." No truthful history of the religious hysteria, frenzy, fanaticism and diabolism of those early days in Utah has ever been written. It was as if civilization had been forced backward four hundred years with the spirit and practice of the Inquisition in full control.

Another condition that added to the frenzy of the "prophets" was the presence of federal officials who attempted to enforce the "common law" in cases of polygamy, and who were regarded as usurpers of the divine right of Brigham Young to be a despot. The conflict between the civil law, represented by the government officials, and the ecclesiastical rule of Brigham Young became so acute that the Gentile officials fled the territory. In order to aid its officials in the enforcement of the law the government, in the spring of 1857, dispatched an army of 2500 men to Utah, which further incensed the Mormon leaders and their followers against the government and against all Gentiles within and without the Mormon empire.

As governor of Utah, and vicegerent of the Mormon deity, Brigham Young issued a proclamation, of which three paragraphs only are necessary:

"Therefore, I, Brigham Young, governor and superintendent of Indian affairs for the Territory of Utah,

"First—Forbid all armed forces of every description from coming into this territory, under any pretense whatever.

"Second—That all the forces in said territory hold themselves in readiness to march at a moment's notice, to repel any and all such invasion.

"Third—Martial law is hereby declared to exist in this territory, from and after the publication of this proclamation; and no person shall be allowed to pass or repass, into or through, or from this territory without a permit from the proper officer."

That the Mormon leaders were determined to make desperate resistance to the entry of the federal troops is proved by the following self-explanatory letter:

"Great Salt Lake City, Sept. 14th, 1857.

"Colonel William. H. Dame, Parowan, Iron county:

"Herewith you will receive the governor's proclamation declaring martial law.

"You will probably not be called out this fall, but are requested to continue to make ready for a big fight another year. The plan of operations is supposed to be about this. In case the United States government should send out an overpowering force, we intend to desolate the territory, and conceal our families, stock and all our effects in the fastnesses of the mountains, where they will be safe, while the men waylay our enemies, attack them from ambush, stampede their animals, take the supply trains, cut off the detachments and parties sent to the canyons for wood, or on other service. To lay waste everything that will burn—houses, fences, fields and grass, so that they cannot find a particle of anything that will be of use to them, not even sticks to make a fire to cook their supplies. To waste away our enemies and to lose none; that will be our mode of warfare. Thus you will see the necessity of preparing, first, secure places in the mountains where they cannot find us, or, if they do, where they cannot approach in force, and then prepare for our families, building some cabins, caching flour and grain. . . . Conciliate the Indians and make them our fast friends.

"In regard to letting the people pass and repass, or travel through the territory, this applies to all strangers and suspected persons. Yourself and Brother Isaac C. Haight, in your districts, are authorized to give such permits. Examine all such persons before giving them such permits to pass. Keep things perfectly quiet, and let all things be done peacefully, but with firmness, and let there be no excitement. Let the people be united in their feelings and faith, as well as works, and keep alive the spirit of reformation. And what we said in regard to saving the grain and provisions we say again. We do not wish to shed a drop of blood if it can be avoided.

"This course will give us great influence abroad.

(Signed)

"BRIGHAM YOUNG (Prophet);

"DANIEL H. WELLS (Lieutenant General).

"Certified to under seal by James Jack, notary public, August 16, 1876."

Brigham Young's letter to Dame is a curious mixture of governor of Utah and king of the Mormon "kingdom of God"—a blending of the civil and ecclesiastic authority, as was intended by the founders of Mormonism.

It should be particularly noted that Bishop Colonel Dame and President Colonel Haight were authorized, as military and ecclesiastical authorities, in their districts, to issue "permits" to "pass or repass" through the territory.

It will be observed that President Young's letter to Dame bears date of September 14, while the date of the proclamation is that of September 15. In the discussion between Haight and John D. Lee on the night of about September 3, it is alleged by the latter that Haight told him that the massacre of the emigrants "is the will of all in authority. The emigrants have no pass from any one to go through the country, and they are liable to be killed as common enemies, for the country is at war now. No man has a right to go through this country without a written pass."

The conversation between Haight and Lee occurred about twelve days before the proclamation is alleged to have been promulgated. President Young received word on the 24th of July, 1857, that Johnston's army was en route to Utah, and it is unbelievable that the astute Brigham would have waited until September 15 to issue his "proclamation" declaring the existence of "martial law."

Under all the circumstances it is not an injustice to charge that, after the massacre, the date of the proclamation was changed from August to September for the purpose of destroying the plain evidence that the massacre of the emigrants was authorized by the proclamation, inasmuch as the emigrants had no "permit" to pass through the territory.

THE DOOMED ARKANSAS COMPANY.

Little is known of the personnel of Fancher's company. No doubt the larger number was from Arkansas. There were many from Missouri, and a few from other states.

William Eaton, whose niece is living in Salt Lake City, was a native of Indiana. During the early fifties he went to Illinois, where he secured a farm. Early in 1857 he met some men from Arkansas who were visiting relatives in Illinois preparatory to moving to California with the Fancher company. Eaton sold his farm, took his wife and little daughter back to Indiana, and joined the company in Arkansas. The last letter received by Mrs. Eaton from her husband stated that all was well, but subsequently she learned that the company had been exterminated.

William A. Aden, another of the victims, was born in Tennessee, and was about twenty years old at the time of the massacre. A recent letter from his brother, James S. Aden of Paris, Henry county, Tennessee, states that his brother was an artist, and relates an interesting incident that occurred in Paris several years prior to his brother's departure for California, and which forms the basis for another interesting incident at Parowan, Utah.

William Laney, a Mormon elder from Utah, was proselyting in the vicinity of Paris. He secured the courthouse and proceeded to expound Mormonism. A number of mischievous lads, among whom was William A. Aden, pushed a small cannon to the rear of the courthouse, and while Elder Laney was preaching the boys discharged the small piece of ordnance. Elder Laney thought that an armed mob was upon him. He abruptly discontinued his discourse, ran from the building and sought safety in hurried flight. On his mad race out of town he met the father of young Aden, who took him home and cared for him during the elder's stay in the vicinity.

Early in 1857 young Aden left Tennessee for California. He sketched scenery along the route, and on his arrival in Utah went on to Provo, about 47 miles south of Salt Lake City, where he did some scenic painting for the Provo Dramatic association. On the arrival of the doomed Arkansas company he joined them and went on to the Mountain Meadows.

Frank E. King and wife traveled with the Fancher company from Pacific Springs, Wyoming, to Salt Lake City, where, owing to the sickness of Mrs. King, he was compelled to remain until December 4, when he went on to Beaver, 210 miles south of Salt Lake City, and thus escaped the fate that lurked for the company in southern Utah.

The author of this story of the massacre is indebted to Mr. Frank E. King for much interesting data relative to the company, and of his experience in Utah about the time of the massacre, and will, therefore, introduce him more fully to the reader.

On Mr. King's arrival in Beaver the bishop of the ward advised him to remain during the winter as the Indians, after the massacre, were more than usually hostile toward Gentiles. Mr. King remained during the winter, and, notwithstanding the friendliness of the bishop, was twice ordered to move on by some of the fanatics. On May 15 Mr. King again started for southern California, and reached Cedar City on the 17th. Quoting from Mr. King's letter, he says:

"I had not unhitched my team when John M. Higbee and Elias Morris, second counselor to Isaac C. Haight, ordered me to leave before the sun rose the next morning."

Mr. King regarded the order as ominous, and returned to central Utah. After living in Manti and other towns he joined the first colony of settlers in Marysvale, Piute county, Utah, where he resided until some five years ago, when he moved to Grant's Pass, Oregon.

Although the writer's intimate acquaintance with Mr. King extended over a period of twenty-five years, I never heard him mention the

Mountain Meadows massacre, and knew nothing of his association with the unfortunate company until his son, Charles, who resides in Marysvale, last winter (1910) told me that his father traveled in Fancher's company. Soon after the discovery I wrote to Mr. King and received some of the information which is used in this history of the massacre.

There were certain questions in dispute, and with my first letter to Mr. King I inclosed a list of questions which, with the answers, are given herewith:

Ques.—Kindly give the names of as many members of the company as you can remember?

Ans.—Fancher, Dunlap, Morton, Haydon, Hudson, Aden, Stevenson, Hamilton, a family by the name of Smith and a Methodist minister.

Ques.—Give the Christian names of the two Dunlap girls and their ages?

Ans.—Rachel and Ruth, aged sixteen and eighteen years, respectively.

Ques.—How many wagons and carriages in the train?

Ans.—Forty.

Ques.—How many men capable of bearing arms, and about how many women—married and single, large girls included?

Ans.—About sixty men, forty women and nearly fifty children.

Ques.—About how many horsemen in the train?

Ans.—About twelve, as near as I can remember.

CONDITIONS IN SOUTHERN UTAH.

The settlements in Iron and Washington counties were less than six years old, and distant 240 to more than 300 miles from Salt Lake City. Mail lines had not been established. All communication with Salt Lake was necessarily by special messenger or by the slower means of those who occasionally went to and fro on business. At the time of which we are writing the people of those remote southern settlements were in the throes of the Mormon "reformation," and the news of the approach of Johnston's army served to intensify the frenzy. They had three years' breadstuff on hand, but were continually urged to husband it for the expected "big fight" with the United States.

PERSONNEL OF THE LEADING ASSASSINS.

Isaac C. Haight resided in Cedar City, about 260 miles southwesterly from Salt Lake City, and forty miles northeasterly from the Mountain Meadows. He was president of the Parowan "stake of Zion," and as such was the ecclesiastical agent in Iron county of President Brigham Young, to whom all the presidents of "stakes" reported, and to whom they were directly responsible for their acts. Haight was also lieutenant colonel in the Iron county militia, and upon him must ever rest the larger part of the odium for the inception and details of the massacre.

As bishop of the Parowan ward of the Parowan "stake of Zion," William H. Dame was under the ecclesiastical direction of President Haight. But as colonel in command of the military district comprising Iron and Washington counties Dame was the military superior of Haight.

John M. Higbee resided in Cedar City, was first counselor to Isaac C. Haight in the Parowan "stake of Zion," and was major in the Iron county militia.

The practice of conferring ecclesiastical, civil and military powers on the same individual has been a distinguishing feature of the Mormon church from its beginning in 1830. Joseph Smith, the founder of Mormonism, was at once the representative of the Mormon god upon the earth, mayor of Nauvoo, and lieutenant general of the Nauvoo legion. And just before his death in 1844, the Mormon "prophet" was nominated for president of the United States by the Democrats under his spiritual control. And it is an inexorable law that the ecclesiastical power of the Mormon hierarchs is superior to that of the civil and military divisions, or adjuncts, of the church.

And there is no doubt that Dame reluctantly became an abettor of butchering the emigrants because of the fact that Haight was his ecclesiastical superior.

There is a popular and widespread impression that John D. Lee was the leader and arch criminal of the massacre. That is not true. He held no special office in the priesthood, but was farmer to the Indians under Superintendent Brigham Young. Lee was a man of medium height, heavy build, and possessed more than average intelligence. As an abject slave of the Mormon priesthood he was a willing tool of his "file leader" in deeds of violence. Lee's father was a member of the "First Families of Virginia," and had not the son become tainted with Mormon superstition, and the victim of the fatuous doctrine of unquestioning obedience to the self-constituted vicegerents of God, he would doubtless have lived and died an honored member of society.

Philip Klingensmith was bishop of the Cedar ward and Samuel McMurdy was his first counselor.

Except in so far as it is necessary in the discussion of the details of the tragedy, it would be an act of wanton cruelty to name the others of the fifty-five white men who were present at the massacre. The public naming of those men would serve no purpose, and would add unnecessary weight to the cross which hundreds of their innocent descendants are bearing.

The great majority of the men who participated in that almost unparalleled crime were not murderers in the generally accepted definition of the word. They were irresponsible victims of gross superstition, and, almost without protest, they stained their souls with blood in the effort to perform the will of God, as they understood the order to commit murder. The execrations of those now living, and of those who will read the story of the tragedy at the Mountain Meadows in the years to come should fall upon those who taught the doctrine of unquestioning obedience and blood atonement, and upon those present day "prophets, seers and revelators" who teach that a Mormon "lies in the presence of God" when he declines to surrender his temporal being to the representatives of an alien and despotic priesthood.

Such were the people, and such were the conditions that awaited Captain Fancher's company of one hundred and fifty souls.

ROUTE OF THE EMIGRANTS.

It was about the middle of August, 1857, when the Arkansas emigrants emerged from Emigration canyon and camped on Emigration square, the present site of the Salt Lake city and county building.

After laying in such supplies as could be obtained in Salt Lake City the emigrants proceeded southward, following the well beaten road that stretched out southerly and then southwesterly to southern California.

According to Mr. Frank E. King the company was short of supplies when they left Salt Lake. At Nephi, about 100 miles south of Salt Lake, they made the attempt to purchase flour of "Red Bill" Black, who ran the flour mill, but were peremptorily refused. A like effort was made at Fillmore, sixty miles south of Nephi, and with like results.

At Corn creek, fourteen miles southwesterly from Fillmore, the emigrants laid over a day or two to permit their work animals and cows which they were taking to California to graze on the then luxuriant pasturage of that locality. During their sojourn at Corn creek one of the emigrants' animals died. A portion of the carcass was eaten by some of the Pahvan Indians, who yet have an encampment near the creek. It is reported that four of the Indians died, presumably from the effects of eating the diseased meat.

That incident has been worn threadbare by Mormon and pro-Mormon historians, who charge that the emigrants poisoned the carcass for the express purpose of killing some of the Indians.

And those same historians also assert that, as an act of revenge, the Indians followed the emigrants to the Meadows and there exterminated them. Those historians also charge that the emigrants poisoned the water of a spring with the purpose, as is alleged, of killing more Indians. The second charge will receive first attention.

The nearest spring is a half mile or more north of where the emigrants were camped, and twice that distance from the old camp ground of the Indians. The spring is in the nature of a slough in soil highly charged with alkali, of which the water contains an appreciable quantity. Not even an Indian would drink the water from that spring while the pure mountain water of Corn creek was within a few rods of where the Pahvans were camped. It would have required many pounds of poison to have been effective on life, and the emigrants would have poisoned their cattle, which were grazing on the bottom land near the slough.

The emigrants were well within that section of Utah where the Indians were periodically at war with the Mormons, and which continued until the close of 1866. The Pahvan tribe was strong and restless. Less than four years previously Moshoquop, the war chief of the Pahvans, and a fraction of his band murdered Lieutenant Gunnison and his exploring party of nearly a dozen men as an act of revenge for the killing of Moshoquop's father by a hot headed emigrant.

The Fancher company was not an aggregation of fools or lunatics. They knew that they were within the power of an enemy that was then preparing for war with the United States. Their failure to obtain food supplies, and the sullen behavior of the Saints would have convinced men of ordinary sense and caution that theirs was a dangerous situation. And they knew that scores of places, like the defile known as Baker's pass, not twenty miles away, where a dozen Indians could waylay and murder a hundred men, must be traversed before they could reach the open country of the Nevada deserts.

And at the second trial of John D. Lee, in 1876, Nephi Johnson, a devout Mormon and Indian interpreter, forever disarmed the lying Mormon historians by declaring that no Pahvan Indians were present at the massacre. A portion of Johnson's evidence, as also that of other witnesses, is given in the appendix at the close of this narrative.

The fact is, western Indians, when pressed for food, eat the flesh of diseased animals; and that the Pahvans knew that the emigrants were blameless in the matter of the death of four of their braves is abundantly proved by the fact that they did not molest the strangers.

At Beaver, about forty-eight miles from Corn creek, the emigrants made another unsuccessful attempt to purchase supplies.

On their arrival at Parowan, thirty miles south from Beaver, the emigrants encamped outside the "fort" or earth wall surrounding the Mormon residences and gardens. By some means the emigrants succeeded in purchasing a small quantity of wheat, but there was no mill in the settlement.

Among those who visited the camp of the emigrants was Elder William Laney, who has before been mentioned as a missionary in Tennessee. William A. Aden immediately recognized Elder Laney as the man whom he, with other boys, had frightened by the discharge of a small cannon in the rear of the courthouse at Paris. Aden at once made himself known to the elder, who recollected that Aden's father had given him shelter when he believed that his life was in danger, and cordially invited the young Tennesseean to visit him within the fort. Aden accepted the elder's hospitality and visited his home where Elder Laney had two wives living in the same cottage. Aden noticed that the elder had a fine patch of onions growing in his front yard and asked to purchase some of them. Elder Laney called his wives and instructed them to pull the onions for Aden. The onions were presented to the son of Laney's benefactor in Tennessee. For that slight act of reciprocal kindness the bishop of Parowan sent two young men by the name of Carter to Laney's house. The latter was called out to the sidewalk where one of the young thugs beat him into insensibility with a club. Laney's wives dragged him into the house and protected him from further assault by the emissaries of the Mormon priesthood. Laney's injuries affected him during the remainder of his life. The incident serves to illustrate the fanaticism and hatred that inspired the Saints to commit the final act of extermination of the emigrants.

From Parowan the road turns sharply to the southwest, and thus continues eighteen miles to Cedar City, where the emigrants made another ineffectual effort to purchase provisions. But Joseph Walker, who was running the flour mills, ground the wheat which had been obtained at Parowan. Bishop Klingensmith sent an elder to Walker and ordered him not to grind the wheat. The sturdy and bluff old Englishman said to the bishop's agent: "Tell the bishop that I have six grown sons, and that we will sell our lives at the price of death to others before I will obey his order." During many weeks after the incident the emissaries of the bishop hounded Walker, and one night while at work in the smutting room of the mill he saved his life by blowing out the candle, thus thwarting the assassins who were lurking near the window of the room. And although Joseph Walker knew by whose orders, and by whom, the Mountain Meadows massacre was perpetrated, he lived and died a Mormon. Once thoroughly converted to the belief that Joseph Smith was a prophet of God, a little thing like the massacre at the Meadows doesn't even jar the faith of the average Mormon.

It is very likely that the emigrants had neglected to apply at Salt Lake City for "permits" to pass through the territory of the United States. They were American citizens, pioneers of Arkansas and Missouri, and were not accustomed to asking for permits to travel the public highways. If defenders of the Mormon "prophets" accept the theory that Brigham Young's "proclamation" declaring martial law was not in effect at the time the emigrants were en route to the Meadows, and that "permits" were not necessary, they abandon the only possible excuse, or apology, for the massacre—that under all the circumstances it was a military necessity, and must, forsooth, concede that it was a religious murder, and that "by their fruits ye shall know them."

Cedar City was the last town on their route to California, and the last place where Brigham Young's order regarding permits could, without a massacre, be enforced. And "Brother" Isaac C. Haight was the last man on the route who was "authorized" by the Mormon "prophet" to issue permits. And there is no doubt that Haight insisted that the orders of his religious master in Salt Lake City be fulfilled to the letter, and that the emigrants resented the insult.

Whether true or false, unfortunately the emigrants cannot be called in rebuttal, the Mormons of Cedar City have been insistent in their charges that the emigrants' conduct was rude, defiant and boisterous. It is alleged that they fired their pistols in the air, "swore like pirates," and defied the town authorities to arrest them. It is also asserted that some of the emigrants from Missouri boasted of having aided in driving the Mormons from that state, and with having helped kill "old Joe Smith" at Carthage jail in Illinois. It is also affirmed that the emigrants swore that they would take provisions by force from the small hamlets and ranches through which they expected to pass on their way down the Santa Clara river.

Fancher's company turned westerly, following the old emigrant trail to California, and camped at the southwest corner of the Cedar co-operative field. According to Mormon statements, it was there that the emigrants committed their last depredation, although they passed through Pinto, six miles northeasterly from the Meadows. According to rumor, they used some fencing for fuel, thus opening the Cedar field to the trespass of range cattle and horses.

The emigrants were then about thirty miles northeasterly from the Meadows. We will precede them and make the reader acquainted with the topography of the locality.

THE MOUNTAIN MEADOWS.

The Mountain Meadows are situated about twenty-five miles southeasterly from Modena, a distributing station on the Salt Lake, Los Angeles & San Pedro railroad, in the southwesterly part of Iron county.

A few miles north of the Washington county line the land rises quite rapidly to the southwesterly "rim of the Great Salt lake basin." Beginning at the "rim," and descending gently toward the southwest some two miles, is a narrow valley or depression similar to scores of others which occur in the higher altitudes of the Rocky mountains. A low, undulating bench, occupied by sparsely growing scrub cedars and pinyon pines, forms the eastern boundary of the depression, while low hills and ridges roll away toward the west a mile or so, where they vanish in the east base of the Beaver Dam range of mountains.

The locality is about 6000 feet above sea level, and fifty years ago the narrow strip of bottom land was covered with luxuriant high altitude grass. With the exception of clumps of scrub oak and scattering cedars on the hillsides, there is nothing to relieve the monotony of the bare hills and ridges. A few springs weakly emerge from the hillsides and bottom land and furnish all the water within a distance of several miles. Well down toward the lower end of the depression a small spring emerged from the sward within about thirty yards to the southeast of where the emigrants went into camp for the last time. To the west, and within twenty rods of the spring, the south end of a low ridge rises from the flat and reaches out a quarter mile or so toward the north. The crest of the ridge is strewn with blocks of basalt, and forms a natural rampart. The base of the eastern hillside is not more than thirty rods from the spring, and is occupied with clumps of oak brush.

About thirty rods northeast of the old camp grounds is a comparatively high hill of small dimensions, from the base of which a low swell, or rise of ground, extends southerly to the bench. To the south and east of the swell, a few rods from its summit, is a depression covered with a dense growth of mountain sage. Across the depression, some thirty rods to the south, the base of the bench is bounded by a gully some twelve feet deep—deeper now than at the time of the massacre. The south side of the gully is conspicuously marked by two large clumps of scrub oak, and beyond the hillside is occupied with sage, scrub oak and scattered cedars. The east clump of oak was the scene of the most terrible incident of all that heartless butchery.

Although the nights were somewhat chilly in the high altitude of the meadows, the days were quite warm, and the emigrants knew that three or four days' travel would take them down into an altitude of about 1500 feet, and out on the blistering sand and gravel strewn plains and mesas of southern Nevada, where, in some localities, the watering places are fifty miles apart, and scant forage for animals. Doubtless those considerations again prompted them to rest their cattle for the hard journey that awaited them. And had conditions been otherwise they were really conserving time and comfort in the delay.

THE CONSPIRACY.

About September 7, or the Sabbath following the departure of the emigrants from Cedar, a meeting of the priesthood was held in the combined school and meeting house on the public square.

There had been hatched in the cruel, priest-ridden brain of Isaac C. Haight a plot to exterminate the emigrants. His scheme was to collect the Indians within a radius of sixty miles and loose them upon the strangers, and he would put the question to the brethren at the meeting. He was already assured of the enthusiastic support of Bishop Klingensmith.

The subject of the extermination of the emigrants was duly presented to the priesthood (nearly every man in the Mormon church holds the priesthood), and was discussed at considerable length. A few of the elders opposed it, while others warmly approved the measure that was so in harmony with the teachings of the "prophets" and with the "spirit of the reformation." The arguments waxed warm and caused considerable commotion.

While the excitement was at its height a commanding figure entered the building. The man was Laban Morrill, who presided over the spiritual and temporal welfare of the Saints at Johnson's Fort, a small settlement about six miles northerly from Cedar. Laban Morrill would have attracted attention anywhere among his fellowmen. His fine head, strong, yet kindly features and dignified bearing marked him as an altogether superior man. After seating himself Mr. Morrill turned to an elder and asked him the cause of the excitement.

After listening a few minutes to the speeches for and against the measure, Laban Morrill arose and dispassionately pointed out the unwisdom and inhumanity of the proposed deed. President Haight and Bishop Klingensmith contended for the perpetration of the infamous crime. They urged that the Lord's prophet had said: "If any miserable curses come here, cut their throats." It was not advice, it was a command. And the emigrants surely came within the meaning of the term "miserable curses." Had they not boasted of having aided in driving the "Lord's chosen people" from Missouri? And had they not also boasted of helping to murder the Lord's greatest prophet, Joseph Smith? And had they not also threatened to raise an army in California and aid in exterminating the Mormons?

Such were the arguments used by Haight, Klingensmith and others to, inflame the passions of the elders, and to "keep alive the spirit of the reformation," as President Young had advised. But the masterful presence of Laban Morrill, for the moment, apparently stood between the emigrants at the Meadows and destruction. The discussion was long and stormy, but Morrill finally forced an apparent compromise. He described the ineffaceable stain that such an infanmy would bring upon the church, and upon the descendants of those who participated in the crime. As a last, and more forcible, argument he told the elders that President Young had not been consulted in the matter. It was then agreed that action be deferred until reply could be received from a message that would be sent the next day to President Young. With that understanding the elders dispersed, and Laban Morrill returned home "feeling," as he subsequently expressed it, "that all was well."

It was nearly dark of an evening some three or four days prior to the priesthood meeting just described, when President Isaac C. Haight walked out on the public square at Cedar City. Evidently he was expecting someone. He had but a few minutes to wait.

A man of medium height, heavy build and square, smooth face rode up and dismounted. After the usual greetings, and a compliment to the newcomer for his promptness in responding to the summons, Haight told Lee that he had an important matter to discuss with him, and suggested that they take some blankets and spend the night in the unused iron works building (subsequently used for a distillery), where they would not be disturbed.

During the night the plot for murdering the emigrants was fully discussed, and the details, so far as possible, were arranged. Nephi Johnson, a youth of nineteen years, and an excellent Indian interpreter, was selected to "stir up" the redskins in the vicinity and send them down to the Meadows. Johnson was to represent to the Indians that the "Mericats"—Gentiles—were at war with the Mormons and Indians, and that the emigrants were going to California with the avowed purpose of returning with an army to exterminate the Mormons and Indians. Carl Shirts, Lee's son-in-law, was assigned to a like mission among the Indians near St. George, and Oscar Hamblin was to lead the Santa Clara Indians to the Meadows.

To those not acquainted with the inner workings of the hierarchal despotism called the Mormon church, it may appear incredible that Nephi Johnson and the others would consent to become tools in a scheme so diabolical, so cruel and inexpressibly treacherous, but the facts to be related will remove the last doubt. Subsquently, Nephi Johnson testified that he was afraid of personal violence if he refused, and that he had known of instances where men had been "injured" for refusal to do as they were told. By an ingenious ruse, at the last moment, Johnson avoided personal participation in the wholesale murder.

The afternoon following the priesthood meeting James H. Haslam, now residing in Wellsville, Cache county, Utah, started on his memorable ride to Salt Lake City, bearing the message of inquiry as to the disposal of the emigrants. The story of that ride, of the relays of horses, of the delay because of the indifference of the bishop of Fillmore, and of other incidents would be interesting, but regard for brevity compels their omission.

THE ATTACK.

In the days of those long and strenuous journeys across the western portion of the continent the emigrants were wont to drive their wagons into a circle with the tongues on the inside for convenience in getting into and out of the wagons. The arrangement served admirably for a fort in case of attack, and formed a corral into which the work animals were driven and held while being yoked or harnessed.

That the emigrants had no suspicion of danger is proved by the haphazard position of their wagons when the first attack was made, and by the other fact that no guards were with their animals. The evidences of the feeling of security aid in disproving the charge that they were guilty of unprovoked acts of aggression and violence in Cedar City.

The morning of September 13 found the men, as usual, early astir. On the east side of the wagons several camp fires were sending up their cheery light, thus relieving the darkness that precedes the early dawn. The forms of men were distinctly outlined against the bright light from burning cedar and sagebrush. There was no premonition of danger. Jets of flame, followed by the cracking of rifles and the fierce warwhoops from the throats of more than a hundred Indians startled the men from their fancied security. Seven men fell dead or mortally wounded. The triumphant yells of the Indians were mingled with the screams of women and the cries of children suddenly awakened to the peril that menaced them. In the excitement, confusion and terror the men secured their arms and, guided by the pandemonium on the hillside, returned the fire with such precision that three Indians were killed and several wounded.

The redskins had been promised an easy victory over the white men, and that none of them would be injured by the "enemies of the Lord." Very naturally, the reds were surprised as well as frightened at the result, and hastily withdrew, carrying with them their dead and injured over the brow of the hill.

The disgusted braves held an impromptu powwow, and immediately dispatched a messenger over the east range to John D. Lee, at Harmony, and his presence demanded at the Meadows. (See appendix.) On Lee's arrival the dead and wounded Indians were pointed out to him as the disastrous results of the attack. According to Lee's statement, the Indians insisted that he at once lead them to victory, or, failing, they would wreak vengeance on the Mormons because of their duplicity in the matter of promised divine protection.

Lee avers that he believed the emigrants had been "sufficiently punished," and that, in order to gain time and to quiet the frenzy of the Indians, who were from Cedar and Parowan, he told them that he would go down to the Santa Clara and hurry up the Indians who were presumed to be en route to the Meadows.

After some parleying Lee was permitted to depart. When some sixteen miles distant he met about one hundred Indians from St. George and the Santa Clara under the direction of Carl Shirts and Oscar Hamblin. With the Indians were some fifteen white men from St. George and the outlying hamlets. As it was then evening the white men went into camp at the upper crossing of the river, while the reds went on to the Meadows.

From Lee's story of the massacre, the truth of which has not been challenged by any defender of the Mormon faith, we are induced to believe that the first intimation that he had that white men were to participate in the butchery was when he met those fifteen men, whom he names, at the upper crossing of the Santa Clara. The camp fire talk of those men removed the last doubt of the intention of the priesthood of the Parowan stake of Zion to blood atone the emigrants. Lee's statement that he spent the night in tears and in supplications to God for some manifestation or sign that the contemplated sacrifice was approved of heaven is at once sincere and pathetic.

EMIGRANTS' HEROIC DEFENSE.

Immediately after the first attack the emigrants drew their wagons into a circle and chained the wheels together. A rifle pit, large enough to protect the women, children and wounded, was dug in the center of the corral. A few feet northeast of the rifle pit a circular excavation about six feet in diameter, and at present about two feet deep, is a pathetic witness that the emigrants made an abortive effort to obtain water by digging, and which remains as evidence of their desperate plight.

During the forenoon of the 14th Lee and the other white men rode from the Santa Clara to the Meadows. Lee immediately sent a dispatch to Haight, which closed as follows: "For my sake, for the people's sake, for God's sake, send me help to protect and save these emigrants."

From a careful analysis of the evidence and statements of those present at the tragedy, and from an inspection of the topography of the Meadows, it is certain that the Indians were camped at a spring about a half mile below the camp of the emigrants, and that the white men camped on the small rivulet to the northeast of "Massacre hill," or in the depression which has been described as being over the "low rise of ground," some fifty to sixty rods northeasterly from the camp of the emigrants.

Some time during the afternoon Lee crossed diagonally over the meadow to the northwest, for the purpose, as he claims, "to take a look at the situation." The emigrants recognized him as a white man, and immediately displayed a white flag. Charley Fancher, son of the captain, and another boy were sent out to interview Lee. But, as he asserts, he hid from the boys, because he had not received word from Haight regarding the final disposal of the emigrants. After a close search for Lee the boys returned to camp. They were not fired upon, which is the only gleam of light in the darkness of the infamous details.

Toward evening the Indians made a detour from their camp to the west, and among the ridges and foothills of the Beaver Dam range approached the basalt ridge to the west and northwest of the improvised fort of the emigrants, and began the second attack on the beleaguered strangers. Lee heard the screams of the women and children, and accompanied by Oscar Hamblin and another man ran across the meadow for the purpose of quieting the redskins. Before reaching the shelter of the ridge, as Lee asserts, he received two bullets through his clothing and one through his hat. The incident has not been disputed by those who appear to think it their duty, in the interest of their church, to blacken the memory of John D. Lee. Aided by Oscar Hamblin Lee quieted the Indians by pleading with them to desist until word could be received from the big Mormon chief at Cedar City.

ASSEMBLING OF WHITE ASSASSINS.

Whether or not Lee's message was received by Haight prior to dispatching a number of the elders to the Meadows is uncertain as well as immaterial. Certain it is that during the 14th William C. Stewart, a high priest and member of the Cedar City council; Bishop Klingensmith, Samuel McMurdy and about thirty-five other white men, under command of Major John M. Higbee, arrived at Leachy spring, in a canyon descending to the east in the range that divides Cedar City from Pinto, and about seventeen miles from the Meadows, where they camped for the night.

Some time during the night of the 13th William A. Aden and two other young men left the camp of the emigrants, and after eluding the white men and Indians started toward Cedar for the purpose, if possible, of obtaining assistance. Arriving at Leachy spring they were challenged by Stewart, to whom Aden stated the nature of their mission. Stewart and another night guard replied with their guns, and the young artist from Tennessee was the first victim of those blood atoning priests, who shot him in the back. One of Aden's companions was wounded, but, with the other emigrant, escaped and succeeded in reaching their camp.

Until the return of Aden's companions no doubt the emigrants hoped that none other than Indians were concerned in the assault upon them. The cowardly murder of Aden was sufficient to convince them that the redskins were merely the allies and tools of the white men, and that they were face to face with annihilation. Even if any of them could escape in the darkness they would surely perish on the desert. Within their inclosure they had buried seven of the brave defenders of the women and children, and others were wounded even then dying. Any attempt to describe the efforts of those heroic men to comfort their wives and to calm the terror of their children would be as fruitless as unprofitable. Out on the desert, with the stars looking down on the final sepulchre of the emigrants, we are compelled to leave them to their reflections. Not until those men, women and children meet their destroyers and the Mormon "prophets" before the bar of eternal justice will the whole truth of the tragedy be known. And not until then will the story of what transpired in the camp of the emigrants be told.

Higbee and his companions arrived at the Meadows the morning after the murder of Aden. Haight's orders were handed to Lee. The nature of those instructions need not be stated. Lee claims that his entire being revolted, but he knew the consequences of refusal.

Why the emigrants did not inclose the spring at the time of forming their corral is inexplicable except on the theory of the excitement that accompanied the attack. Prior to the 15th they secured water during the night time. It appears, however, that on the 15th the supply was exhausted. Two men went out to the spring, and while a rain of lead spattered around them, filled their pails and reached the fort in safety. On another occasion two men went out after wood and, while the bullets whistled by and tore up the ground around them, coolly chopped the wood and returned to the inclosure. The foregoing is the tribute paid to the courage of those men by John D. Lee. That those shots were fired from the top of Massacre hill, within fifteen rods of the Mormon camp, is proved by the fact that the spring was sheltered from attack from miscreants on the ridge to the northwest by the intervening wagons, and the other fact that all other points were unprotected from the return fire of the emigrants.

The evening of the 15th again witnessed the assembling of the Indians behind the basalt ridge. Again they poured volley after volley into the improvised fort, and were answered with energy and precision. One of the Santa Clara Indians was killed and three others were wounded. Disgusted with the second failure of divine protection, some of the reds rounded up a bunch of the emigrants' cattle and returned to their camp on the Santa Clara river.

The Mormons were astir early on the morning of the 16th. The ruddy glow of a dozen camp fires lighted up the small depression and cast weird shadows as the men walked to and fro or squatted around the fires while preparing the morning meal.

While yet dark the men were summoned to prayers. Under the blue vault of heaven, from which the angels must have looked down with infinite sorrow on the hellish scene, those wretched victims of unquestioning obedience, of superstition and fanaticism, knelt in the form of a "prayer circle." With heads bowed in abject servility to an alien god, and each right arm raised in the form of a square, those unhappy dupes listened while one of the "servants of the Lord" asked the blessing of their god upon the deeds they were about to enact, and for divine protection while they were "avenging the blood of the prophets who died in Carthage jail," and the martyrs who perished in Missouri and Illinois. The invocation ended, the brethren convened in "council."

It has ever been the boast of the Mormon priesthood that all questions of importance to the church are submitted to the Saints and are decided by "common consent," and which, being interpreted, means consenting to the will of the Mormon god's vicegerents, or, failing, they "lie in the presence of God." And because of that rule the "council meeting," convened for the ostensible purpose of debating the measures embraced in Haight's program for the disposal of the emigrants was a burlesque. The fate of the emigrants had been predetermined by Isaac C. Haight, who was the direct agent of the "holy" vicegerents who resided at Salt Lake. The "council" was merely a ratification meeting. Some there were who had the courage to oppose the infamous measures, but their voices were feeble in the presence of "the leading priesthood."

Jacob Hamblin, brother of Oscar Hamblin, and a trusted missionary to the Indians, owned a ranch some two miles northeasterly from the Meadows, and near the junction of the roads from Modena and Cedar City to the Meadows. At the time of the massacre Hamblin was not at home. But Samuel Knight, from the Santa Clara, was temporarily ranching near the Hamblin place. During the forenoon of the 16th a messenger arrived at Hamblin's and requested Knight to go with his team over to the Meadows. Knight must have known of the attack on the emigrants, and very likely suspected the reason for the request. He pleaded the illness of his wife. The request was then made for the use of his team. Knight explained that his horses were only partly broken, and that if the demand were imperative he would go with them. Such, in brief, was Knight's testimony at the second trial of Lee.

THE MASSACRE.

Unless it was the natural dread that nearly all men feel when conscience rebels at the vision of treachery and carnage, there is no explanation of the postponement of the final arrangements for the massacre until 2 p. m. At about that hour William Bateman, carrying a white flag, and accompanied by Lee, appeared on the low rise of ground which separated the camp of the Mormons from that of the emigrants. Bateman went on to within a short distance of the corral, where he paused and awaited some sign of recognition. A man named Hamilton went out to Bateman, and after a short parley the former returned to the corral. Within a few minutes Hamilton again went out and told Bateman that the emigrants would put themselves under the protection of the flag of truce. Bateman waved his flag, and the curtain was lifted on one of the most inexcusable and atrocious crimes of all the centuries.

Lee hastened down to the corral, followed by two teams driven by McMurdy and Knight. The emigrants drew aside one of their wagons, thus opening the corral. McMurdy, followed by Knight, drove into the inclosure. The emigrants were burying two men who had just died of their wounds. Conditions within the camp can best be described in the words of John D. Lee.

"As I entered the fortifications, men, women and children gathered around me in wild consternation. Some felt that the time of their happy deliverance had come, while others, although in deep distress, and all in tears, looked upon me with doubt, distrust and terror." Describing his sensations, Lee continues: "My position was painful, trying and awful; my brain seemed to be on fire; my nerves were for a moment unstrung; humanity was overpowered, as I thought of the cruel, unmanly part I was acting. . . . I knew that I was acting a cruel part and doing a damnable deed. Yet my faith in the godliness of my leaders was such that it forced me to think that I was not sufficiently spiritual to act the important part I was commanded to perform. . . . I delivered my message, and told the people that they must put their arms in the wagon, so as not to arouse the animosity of the Indians. I ordered the children and wounded, some clothing and arms, to be put into the wagons." In speaking of the defensive condition of the camp, Lee says: "If the emigrants had had a good supply of ammunition they never would have surrendered, and I do not think we could have captured them without great loss, for they were brave men and very resolute and determined."

Continuing, Lee says:

"Just as the wagons were loaded (Adjutant) Dan McFarland (of St. George) came riding into the corral and said that Major Higbee had ordered great haste to be made, for he was afraid the Indians would return and renew the attack before he could get the emigrants to a place of safety."

In the meantime the militia, nearly fifty in number, moved over the low ridge and proceeded close down to the emigrant camp and, in single file and about six feet apart, took positions on the southeast side of the road.

The Indians, some two hundred strong, secreted themselves in the rank sage and behind cedar trees in the near vicinity of the Mormon camp.

Nephi Johnson's horse had learned the trick of untying his halter rope when it was carelessly fastened. Johnson, as I have been informed by his intimate friends, carelessly tied his horse to a cedar tree, then stepped back and watched the intelligent brute untie the knot and scamper up the hillside to the south. Johnson obtained permission from Major Higbee to go after his horse, and took a position on the point of the bench from which he had an unobstructed view of the entire field.

Two wounded men and a number of children, "too young to tell tales," were placed in Knight's wagon which emerged from the corral preceded by Lee and McMurdy's wagon. Following Knight's wagon were the women and children old enough to "tell tales." When the women reached a point about one hundred yards northeasterly from the corral, the male emigrants, in single file, and about six feet apart, were permitted to begin the line of march. When they were opposite the militia the latter stepped forward and, keeping a few feet to the right of the emigrants, joined in the death march—following the women and children.

The horses driven by Samuel McMurdy were unusually fast walkers, and Lee, who had charge of the first division of the emigrants—the women and children, was forced to repeatedly admonish McMurdy not to travel so rapidly. The respective localities had been carefully selected for the slaughter of the men and women, and it would not do to have McMurdy pass the point where the Indians were secreted until the word was given to begin the carnage. The arrangements were made and carried out with all the precision of a legalized execution.

There can be not the slightest doubt that the men knew the meaning of the peculiar formation of the procession. If there were danger of an attack by the Indians why was it, they thought, that they were not permitted to retain their firearms and aid in the protection of their wives and children? But, through unparalleled treachery, they were then powerless, and there was probably the hope that those so dear to them might be spared. That no word of protest was spoken is the strongest commendation of their heroism and evidence of their resignation.

Major Higbee was mounted and occupied a position on the summit of the low elevation over which the wagons and women and children must pass. The advance section of the procession passed over the elevation and were partially, if not entirely, hidden from those in the rear, when Higbee gave the command: "Do your duty!"

Terrified by the explosion of firearms and yells of the Indians, Knight's horses reared and plunged. He leaped from the wagon, caught his horses by the bits, and turned his face from the awful scene.

One of the wounded men in Knight's wagon was holding his companion in his arms. While Knight was quieting his frightened horses McMurdy ran to Knight's wagon, raised his gun and exclaimed:

"O, Lord, my God, receive their spirits: it is for thy kingdom that I do this!" The gun exploded and the bullet killed both men. Samuel McMurdy had surely "kept alive the spirit of the reformation"; he had vindicated his right to hold the "holy" Mormon priesthood, and to be first counselor to Bishop Klingensmith.

According to Nephi Johnson less than three minutes were consumed in the work of death.

During the excitement and confusion attending the massacre, two girls, Rachel and Ruth Dunlap, made a desperate attempt to escape the carnage. From the evidence, and from a careful study of the ground, the girls must have been on the north side of the group of women and children when the attack was made. Running to the east on the north side of Knight and McMurdy's wagons, they turned to the south and sped toward the bench, where clumps of oak bushes seemed to invite them to a temporary refuge. Clambering down the steep side of the gully they crept into the oaks on the opposite brink. They were then about thirty rods from the scene of death, over which the smoke from exploding firearms hung in a hazy cloud from which there no longer issued protesting cries of women and the pitiful screams of children.

During a few brief minutes Rachel and Ruth Dunlap believed they were saved from the white and red butchers. Very likely no thought entered their minds of the fate that awaited them on the desert—the thirst and hunger that surely lurked for them amid the inextricable maze of hills and desert canyons. They dreamed not that if they escaped to some habitation the occupants, under pain of death, must surrender them to the blood atoning priests because, forsooth, they were old enough to tell the story of the massacre. Their only hope was to see the setting of the sun and to feel the sheltering mantle of night descend upon them.

One or more of the assassins must have seen the terrified girls as they raced toward the gully and reported the fact to the chief from Parowan, who found the girls and dragged them from their hiding place. The Indian sent for Lee, and on his arrival asked what should be done with them. When informed that they were beyond the age limit prescribed by Haight, the chief pleaded that they were "too pretty to be killed." Divining the sentence pronounced by Lee, the elder girl dropped to her knees and with clasped hands cried out: "Spare me, and I will love you all my life!" But she died, as her sister had died, and at Lee's hands. (Lee vehemently denied the awful charge.) For pitiful story of attempt by Hamblin's Indian boy to save the girls, see appendix.

Note.—Since the massacre, rumors have been persistent to the effect that prior to their death those girls were outraged by those who murdered them. The charge was so terrible, so diabolical and inhuman that, as a Mormon, and later on an "apostate," I could not believe the rumor—it appeared to be just another Mormon canard to further blacken the memory of John D. Lee. There was, however, something in the terms of the girl's appeal that is inexplicable when considered apart from the rumor. Last winter (1910) I met a devout Mormon woman in southern Utah, who was a girl at the date of the massacre, and she assured me that the rumor is entirely trustworthy; that she remembers hearing the women of St. George discuss the awful fate of the Dunlap girls. "And," the lady concluded "we Mormons have never been accused of charging crimes to our people when the accusations were not true."

Jacob Hamblin was on his way from Salt Lake to his ranch near the Meadows when the massacre was perpetrated. Hamblin's Indian boy, Albert, who was about sixteen years old, and whom the former had adopted, was present at the massacre and witnessed the ravishment of the Dunlap sisters and the cutting of their throats. On Hamblin's arrival at the ranch the boy conducted him to the clump of oak brush where the bodies of the girls, nude and bloated, furnished ghastly evidence of the truth of the young Indian's story. Subsequently, Hamblin interviewed the Indian chief, who was Lee's partner in that special crime, and who verified the young redskin's story, and repeated the words used by the elder girl when pleading for her life.

The above is the substance of Hamblin's testimony on that incident as given at Lee's second trial.

We will draw the curtain on the scene, leaving those religion-crazed fanatics to the judgment of a merciful God, and the logic and lessons to the public.

On the old camp ground of the emigrants Major Carleton of the United States army and other kindly hands reared a monument of boulders which cover the remains of Captain Fancher and his company, which, the spring following the massacre, were buried by Jacob Hamblin in the rifle pit digged by the emigrants. Major Carleton also erected a rude cross upon which he carved the legend: "Vengeance is mine, and I will repay, saith the Lord." Some miscreant destroyed the cross. Easterly and westerly the monument is about twelve feet long by six feet wide. The west end is now about four feet high, and the east end is a foot or so above the ground. From the east end of the grave the earth descends to the bottom of a deep gully, made by floods during recent years, and unless protective measures are soon taken the spring and summer floods will eat away the last visible evidence of the Mountain Meadows massacre.

The once carpet of grass has vanished, and in its place is a dense growth of mountain sage. The spring that supplied the Fancher company with water now oozes up from a bog near the bottom of the gully. And all around the landscape is an indescribable desolation a vista of gray sage and barren hills. Seemingly, the God of Justice has visited the locality with the withering blight of his displeasure but Mormonism yet lives, aggressive, arrogant and defiant.

As the occasional visitor, with bared head, stands by the desert grave, his imagination recalls the death march up the valley. Through the silence of more than fifty years is heard the echoes of exploding firearms. The shrieks of women and children mingle with the frenzied cries of fiends incarnate, then the death like silence returns. He seems to feel the touch of spirit hands, to hear the murmur of spirit voices pleading for remembrance of their wrongs, and for human justice for the false and criminal leaders of the system whose doctrines and example inspired their destruction, and who continue to traduce their victims as their only defense of the ruthless murder of those who surrendered under the sacred aegis of the flag of peace!

FURTHER DETAILS—FROM MAJOR CARLETON'S REPORT.

Prior to the publication of the foregoing story of the massacre repeated efforts were made to obtain a copy of Maj. J. H. Carleton's report of the tragedy made to the war department during the spring of 1859. Each effort was fruitless until the 29th of this month, when, by a fortunate incident, it was learned where the loan of a copy could be obtained.

In the compilation of the material from which the major made his report it became necessary to interview leading Mormons then residing in southern Utah; among whom was Jacob Hamblin, who has been sufficiently introduced to the reader. And inasmuch as the participants in the massacre had been enjoined to "keep silent" on the subject, and all Mormons were interested in shielding their "brethren" and their church from the odium of the crime, it was impossible to obtain the truth. As has been proved by Jacob Hamblin's evidence in the second trial of Lee, he knew every important detail of the crime, but in his interview with Major Carleton he placed the entire responsibility for the tragedy upon the Indians. When the latter were interviewed they denied the responsibility, but, like their Mormon friends, they were reticent as to the details of the crime and the identity of the participants.

It was only by analysis of the testimony of the Mormons and Indians whom the major interviewed, and noting the numerous contradictions, that he was able to justly charge the crime to the Mormon priesthood of southern Utah. Under such conditions it is a marvel that Major Carleton was able to sufficiently unravel the entangled web of falsehoods to enter even upon the confines of accuracy. Every important detail of the major's report, not given in the text of this story of the massacre, is given in the following excerpta, which will be highly appreciated because of the additional information regarding the personnel of the seventeen children saved from the slaughter.

The Author, October 31, 1910.

The Muddy river branch of the Pahute Indians, now residing on the reservation near Moapa, on the Salt Lake, Los Angeles & San Pedro railroad, were a murderous lot of savages at the time of the massacre. That, and the additional fact that their headquarters were more than 150 miles from the Mountain Meadows, doubtless induced the Mormons to implicate the Muddy Indians in the crime. During his determined efforts to get at the facts Major Carleton interviewed prominent men of that division of the Pahutes. They replied as follows:

"Where are the wagons, the cattle, the clothing, the rifles, and other property belonging to the train? We have not got or had them. No; you will find these things in the hands of the Mormons."

While camping at the Mountain Meadows, May, 1859, Major Carleton interviewed Mrs. Jacob Hamblin, who lived within two or three miles of the Meadows at the time of the massacre. Following is the major's report of the interview:

"Mrs. Hamblin is a simple minded person of about 45, and evidently looks with the eyes of her husband at everything. She may really have been taught by the Mormons to believe it is no great sin to kill Gentiles and enjoy their property. Of the shooting of the emigrants, which she herself had heard, and knew at the time what was going on, she seemed to speak without a shudder, or any very great feeling; but when she told of the seventeen orphan children who were brought by such a crowd to her house of one small room there in the darkness of the night, two of the children cruelly mangled, and the most of them with their parents' blood still wet upon their clothes, and all of them shrieking with grief and terror and anguish, her own heart was touched. She at least deserves kind consideration for her care and nourishment of the three sisters (Rebecca, Louisa and Sarah Dunlap, the younger sisters of

Rachel and Ruth Dunlap, whose pitiful fate has been detailed), and for all she did for the little girl, about 1 year old, who had been shot through one of her arms, below the elbow, by a large ball, .breaking both bones and cuting the arm half off."

A few of the children saved from the slaughter were subsequently taken to the Indian farm at Corn creek, where, it is asserted, the emigrants had poisoned the water. One of those girls, named Elsie, so it is credibly reported, remained at Corn creek and later on became the wife of a highly respected stockman—a gentleman who was widely known in Utah. The other sixteen children were taken to Salt Lake City and delivered to Dr. Forney, United States Indian agent, who sent them to their relatives in Arkansas and other states. Of the personnel of the children Major Carleton reported as follows:

Sixteen of those were seen by Judge Cradlebaugh, Lieutenant Kearney, and others, and gave the following information in relation to their personal identity, etc. The children varied from 3 to 9 years of age, ten girls, six boys, and were questioned separately. The first is a boy named Calvin, between 7 and 8 years; does not remember his surname; says he was by his mother when she was killed, and pulled the arrows from her back until she was dead; says he had two brothers older than himself, named James and Henry, and three sisters, Mary, Martha and Nancy.

"The second is a girl who does not remember her name. The others say it is Demurr.

"The third is a ,boy named Ambrose Miriam Tagit; says he had two brothers older than himself and one younger. His father, mother and two elder brothers were killed; his younger brother was brought to Cedar City; says he lived in Johnston county, but does not know what state; says it took one week to go from where he lived to his grandfather's and grandmother's, who are still living in the states.

"The fourth is a girl obtained from John Morris, a Mormon, at Cedar City. She does not recollect anything about herself.

"Fifth, a boy obtained from E. H. Grove; says the girl obtained from Morris is named Mary and is his sister.

"The sixth is a girl who says her name is Prudence Angelina; had two brothers, Jesse and John, who were killed. Her father's name was William, and she had an uncle Jesse.

"The seventh is a girl. She says her name is Frances Harris, or Horne; remembers nothing of her family.

"The eighth is a boy too young to remember anything about himself.

"The ninth is a boy whose name is William W. Huff.

"The tenth is a boy whose name is Charles Francher" (Fancher).

(Note,—Charles Fancher was the son of Capt. Charles Fancher, who was in command of the train, and was 11 years old. He was small for his age. He had a brother about 9 years of age, who was also small for his years, and which, no doubt, was the reason for their escape from the fate of those who were believed to be over 8 years old. Mormon children are baptised at 8 years, when, from the Mormon viewpoint, they reach the age of responsibility. Thus it was that the emigrant children under 8 years were not regarded by the Mormon priests as being responsible for the sins of their parents, who were murdered in obedience to the endowment oath to "avenge the blood of the (Mormon) prophets and martyrs." It was from the lips of Charley Fancher, soon after his arrival from the vicinity of the tragedy, that I heard the first story of the massacre. In his childish way he said that "some of the Indians, after the slaughter, went to the little creek, and that after washing their faces they were white men." During his stay in Salt Lake City I frequently played marbles with Charley Fancher on First South, a half block or so west of Main street.—The Author.)

"The eleventh is a girl who says her name is Sophronia Huff.

"The twelfth is a girl who says her name is Betsy.

"The thirteenth, fourteenth and fifteenth are three sisters named Rebecca, Louisa and Sarah Dunlap. These three sisters were the children obtained from Jacob Hamblin.

"I have no note of the sixteenth.

"The seventeenth is a boy who was but 6 years old at the time of the massacre. Hamblin's wife brought him to my camp on the 19th instant. The next day they took him on to Salt Lake City to give him up to Dr. Forney. He is a pretty little boy and hardly dreamed he had again slept on the ground where his parents had been murdered."

It was twenty months after the massacre when Major Carleton encamped on the Meadows. His description of conditions will be interesting. He said:

"The scene of the massacre, even at this late day, was horrible to look upon. Women's hair, in detached locks and masses, hung to the sage bushes and was strewn over the ground in many places. Parts of little children's and of female costumes dangled from the shrubbery or lay scattered about."

From Major Carleton's statement of the number of skulls and other human bones which he gathered up and buried, it is evident that Jacob Hamblin's statement of the number of skeletons which he collected and buried was exaggerated, or that there were many more people in the company than has been heretofore estimated. And some of the bones were found a mile or so from the old camp ground, at points to which the coyotes had dragged them.

TRIAL AND EXECUTION OF JOHN D. LEE.

During the year 1875 Lee was tried for his part in the massacre. There were seven Mormons and five Gentiles on the jury. It was a mistrial. The Gentiles voted for conviction, the Mormons for acquittal. The wave of indignation that swept over the United States convinced the Mormon leaders that at least one Mormon must be sacrificed in the interest of their church. Haight and Higbee were hiding in the wilds of Arizona or Mexico. Klingensmith had taken refuge with a band of Indians in Arizona at a place on the south side of the Colorado river, opposite Eldorado canyon, in southern Nevada, where he took unto himself a squaw as his fourth or fifth wife. He voluntarily became a witness for the people during the first trial of Lee. He saved his neck, but lied with such facility that his evidence was of no value to the government, and after his discharge he returned to his wickiup on the Colorado.

The second trial of Lee occurred in September, 1876. The Mormon witnesses that could not be found during the first trial were easily located for the second trial, and became eager witnesses on every feature of the evidence that was necessary to convict John D. Lee. But the attorneys for the government found it impossible to awaken the slumbering memories of the elders of any evidence that would convict others of the assassins.

Another significant feature of the trial was that the marshal who subpoenaed the jurors must have received a "hunch," for he secured as many Mormon jurors as the law permitted.

It was believed by the marshal who had charge of the arrangements for Lee's execution that if the Mountain Meadows were selected as the place for the final ordeal that the condemned man might, on the tragic ground, be induced to make a statement of the inside facts which would enable the representatives of the government to work more intelligently in the matter of bringing other guilty men to justice.

It was about 10 a. m., March 23, 1877, when Lee and his executioners arrived at the Meadows. Photographer James Fennemore of Beaver, where Lee was tried; Josiah Rogerson, a Mormon telegrapher; a number of newspaper correspondents, including S. A. Kenner of the Deseret News, and a small number of spectators were present.

Prior to the execution Lee accompanied the marshal and a number of those present over the field and pointed out the respective localities of chiefest interest. But no useful information was divulged.

Lee's coffin was brought from the wagon and placed near the mound of stones which cover the remains of the emigrants.

A covered wagon was drawn up to within a few paces of the coffin. Five holes had been made in the cover, and five men were seen to disappear within the wagon.

Standing near his final receptacle, Lee made a brief farewell speech in which he denied any intent to do wrong. He claimed, and rightly, too, that he had been betrayed—sacrificed in the interest of the church to which he had given his whole life. Continuing, the doomed man said:

"Still, there are thousands of people in this church that are honorable and good hearted friends, some of whom are near to my heart. There is a kind of living, magnetic influence which has come over the people, and I cannot compare it to anything else than the reptile that enamores its prey till it captivates it, paralyzes it, and it rushes into the jaws of death. I cannot compare it to anything else. It is so. I know it. I am satisfied of it."

Lee's vision swept the scene of former carnage. He looked out on the repulsive ridge from which had been poured the deadly missiles into the emigrant camp. Furtively he glanced at the monument erected by Major Carleton. Mortals will never know the thoughts that, with torrential confusion, leaped through the brain of the doomed man as he sat down on his coffin for the crucial ordeal. He asked that his arms be not pinioned, and that his eyes be not bandaged. The first request was granted. United States Marshal William Nelson fastened a handkerchief over Lee's eyes, then stepped to one side. Lee clasped his hands over his head and said to the marshal: "Let them shoot the balls through my heart! Don't let them mangle my body!"

The marshal called "Ready, aim, fire!" A sharp, simultaneous explosion, and the victim of unquestioning obedience had paid the mortal demand for vengeance, had satisfied the doctrine of human justice!

Lee was the husband of nineteen wives, one of whom, however, was a "spiritual" wife. By eighteen of his wives he had sixty-four children, fifty-four of whom were living at the time of his death.

His last wife, Ann Gorge, was married to him by Heber C. Kimball about 1865, which created considerable gossip among the Saints of southern Utah where every incident of the massacre was well known. And it will be proved by the evidence of Jacob Hamblin, given at Lee's second trial, that Brigham Young and his second counselor, George A. Smith, knew every detail of the massacre which was known to Jacob Hamblin, and he knew all of the facts and the name of every prominent participant within a very short time after the occurrence of the tragedy.

At the time of Lee's interview, on September 29, as proved in the appendix herewith, Lee told President Young that there was "not a drop of innocent blood in the company" of emigrants. If no "innocent blood" was shed at the Meadows, under the "revelation" on plural marriage given to the first "prophet," then was John D. Lee and the other assassins guiltless before the Mormon god, and there was no obstacle in the way of Lee and Haight taking more plurals after the massacre, and becoming members of the Utah legislature. Indeed, the addition to their harems of more plurals was, according to the polygamy "revelation," a certain means of salvation and exaltation. Under the teachings of that "revelation" the debauching and murder of the Dunlap girls was no bar to the highest exaltation in the Mormon "celestial kingdom of God"! Paragraph 26 of the "revelation" reads as follows:

"Verily, verily I say unto you (Joseph Smith), if a man marry a wife (or wives) according to my word, and they are sealed by the holy spirit of promise, according to mine appointment, and he or she shall commit any sin or transgression of the new and everlasting covenant whatever, and all manner of blasphemies, and if they commit no murder, wherein they shed innocent blood—yet shall they come forth in the first resurrection, and enter into their exaltation. . . ."

For further details and particulars regarding the culpability of the leaders of the Mormon church, the reader is respectfully referred to the appendix herewith.

APPENDIX.

Laban Morrill moved from Johnson's fort and became one of the pioneers of Piute county, settling at Junction, now the county seat. He died some ten or fifteen years ago, leaving a large family which, like their father, is highly respected.

At the second trial of Lee, and after the usual preliminaries, Mr. Morrill testified as follows:

"We had formed a kind of custom to come together about once a week, to take into consideration what would be the best good for those places. I happened on Sunday (about September 7) to come to Cedar City, as I usually came, and there seemed to be a council. We met together about 4 o'clock, as a general thing, on Sunday evening after service. I went into the council and saw there a little excitement in regard to something I did not understand. I went in at a rather late hour. I inquired of the rest what the matter was. They said a company had passed along toward Mountain Meadows. There were many threats given concerning this company.

"As I said, there appeared to be some confusion in that council. I inquired in a friendly way, what was up. I was told that there was an emigrant train that passed along down near Mountain Meadows, and that they had made threats in regard to us as a people—said they would destroy every d—d Mormon. There was an army coming on the south and north, and it created some little excitement. I made two or three replies in a kind of debate measure that were taken into consideration, discussing the object, what method we thought best to take in regard to protecting the lives of the citizens.

"My objections were not coincided with. At last we touched upon the topic like this: We should still keep quiet, and a dispatch should be sent to Governor Young to know what would be the best course. The vote was unanimous. I considered it so. It seemed to be the understanding that on the coming morning, or the next day, there should be a messenger dispatched. I took some pains to inquire and know if it would be sent in the morning. The papers were said to be made out, and Governor Young should be informed, and no hostile course pursued until his return. I returned back to Fort Johnson, feeling that all was well. About eight and forty hours before the messenger returned— business called me to Cedar City, and I learned that the job had taken place. I can't give any further evidence on the subject at present."

W. W. Bishop, counsel for Lee, elicited the information from Mr. Morrill that when he referred to "the job" he meant the killing of the emigrants. United States District Attorney Howard then put the following re-direct questions:

Ques.—Did you say that a messenger was to be sent down to John D. Lee?

Ans.—I did, but I did not see him start. I understood at the time a messenger was to be sent.

Ques.—What did you understand?

Ans.—I understood there was to be word sent down towards Pinto creek.

Ques.—For what purpose?

Ans.—To have the thing stayed according to contract, to agreement made.

Ques.—What do you mean by the thing being stayed? Was the massacre of that emigrant train discussed there at all?

Ans.—It was, sir; and some were in favor of it, and some were not.

Ques.—Who were they?

Ans.—Bishop Smith (Klingensmith) I considered, was the hardest man I had to contend with.

Ques.—Who else spoke about it?

Ans.—Isaac Haight and one or two others. I recollect my companions more than any one else.

Ques.—They were very anxious and rabid were they not?

Ans.—They seemed to think it would be best to kill the emigrants. Some of the emigrants swore that they had killed old Joseph Smith; there was quite a little excitement there.

Ques.—You have given us the names of two who were in favor of killing those emigrants—who were the others?

Ans.—Those were my companions, Isaac C. Haight and Klingensmith. I recollect no others:

And who after reading the testimony of Laban Morrill, and noting his sincerity under the most trying conditions—to tell the truth, and to shield others of the elders, can deny that the conspiracy to murder the emigrants was initiated by the direct agent of the Mormon leaders, and was discussed in a priesthood meeting of the chief ecclesiastical authorities of the Parowan stake of Zion?

Question by Howard—Who else did he mention?

Ans.—He mentioned my brother (Oscar Hamblin) being there, bringing some Indians there. Sent him word of this affair (the massacre) taking place, and for him to go and get the Indians, and bring up the Santa Clara Indians.

Ques.—Your brother, then, brought the Indians to the Meadows, and then left there?

Ans.—Yes, he told me so. (The fact is, if Oscar Hamblin left the Meadows after taking the Indians there, he returned and aided Lee in restraining them when they made their second attack on the emigrants.)

Question by bishop—Have you ever given a report of it (the massacre) to any of your superiors in the church, or officers over you?

Ans.—Well, I did speak of it to President Young and George A. Smith.

Ques.—Did you give them the whole facts?

Ans.—I gave them more than I have here, because I recollected more of it.

Ques.—When did you do that?

Ans.—Pretty soon after it happened.

Ques.—You are certain that you gave it fuller than you have told it here on the stand?

Ans.—I told everything I could.

Ques.—Have you told it all?

Ans.—No, sir, I have not.

Ques.—Then tell it.

Ans.—I will not undertake that now. I would not like to undertake it.

Question by Bishop—State whether you were under any compulsion (to go to the Meadows).

Ans.—I didn't think it was safe for me to object.

Ques.—Explain what you mean, that is what I want. Where was the danger—who was the danger to come from if you objected—from Haight or those around him—from the Indians, or from the emigrants?

Ans.—From the military officers.

Ques.—Where?

Ans.—At Cedar City.

Ques.—Was Haight one of those military officers?

Ans.—Yes, sir.

Ques.—Who was the highest military officer in Cedar City at that time?

Ans.—I think it was Isaac C. Haight.

Ques.—You thought it would not be safe to refuse; had you any reason to fear danger has any person ever been injured for not obeying, or anything of that kind?

Ans.—I don't want to answer.

Ques.—It is necessary to the safety of the man I am defending, and I therefore insist upon an answer. Had any person been injured for not obeying?

Ans.—Yes, sir, they had.

Question by Howard—Were you acquainted with the Indians—the Pah Vant (Pahvan) Indians?

Ans.—Yes, sir; somewhat acquainted.

Ques.—Were any of the Pah Vant Indians down there?

Ans.—I didn't see any.

During the night of the day of the massacre President Isaac C. Haight and Bishop William H. Dame arrived from Cedar and Parowan, respectively, and camped at Hamblin's ranch. The next morning, with John D. Lee, they visited the scene of the carnage where sixty men, forty women and about thirty children were lying naked on the ground, having been stripped of their clothing and jewelry.

Haight, Dame and other leading elders made speeches, the substance of which may be gathered from answers by Nephi Johnson to questions asked by W. W. Bishop, Lee's attorney.

Ques.—Is it not a fact that after the property was all gathered up at the Meadows, and you were ready to start for Iron Springs, that speeches were made to the men present, by those in authority, in which speeches you were ordered to keep it a secret forever?

Ans.—There were a great many speeches made.

Ques.—At the Meadows, before you left there, was it not told you in a speech then made to you, that it must be kept a secret; that it would be best to keep silent? Were not you so advised by your leaders?

Ans.—Yes, sir.

IN DEFENSE OF THE EMIGRANTS.

In reply to my inquiry of Frank E. King as to the conduct of the people who were traveling in the Fancher company, he replied, under date of March 15, 1910, as follows:

"From the time that we overtook them (at Pacific Springs) they were not boisterous, or in any way uncivil. You would hardly ever hear an oath from any one."

Although to the point, Mr. King's replies were brief, as he always was in his intercourse with his fellow men.

The following affidavit is self explanatory:

"State of Utah, County of Piute—ss.

"William L. Jones, Reuben De Wit, George T. Henry and Josiah F. Gibbs, being first duly sworn, and each for himself, deposes and says: We are residents of Marysvale, Piute county, Utah. And that during our residence in Marysvale we were personally acquainted, during a period of more than twenty years, with Frank E. King who, until about five years ago, was also a resident of Marysvale, Piute county, and that the said Frank E. King was an industrious, upright citizen, and of unquestioned veracity.

(Signed)   "WILLIAM L. JONES, (ex-Postmaster.)

"REUBEN DE WIT, (Justice of the Peace.)

"GEORGE T. HENRY, (Postmaster.)

"JOSIAH F. GIBBS.

Subscribed and sworn to before me, tris 15th day of August, 1910.

"WILLIAM E. WHITE, Notary Public.

"My commission expires March 16, 1913."

An estimable lady (a Mrs. Evans), yet living at Parowan, visited the camp of the emigrants at Parowan with other Mormon girls, and is earnest in her statement that in every respect the emigrants conducted themselves as ladies and gentlemen. Her statement was made to a gentleman of high repute in the official life of Utah, and is published without the knowledge of either of them.

The charge that the emigrants resisted arrest at Cedar clearly proves that they declined to ask for permits, and for which the inexpressibly detestable ecclesiastical tyrant, Isaac C. Haight, commanded their arrest. The demand was made by the emissaries of a fanatical and brutalized priesthood that was then in open rebellion against the United States. In resisting arrest by the servile agents of the Mormon "prophets," because they ignored the right of bigots and rebels to prevent them from passing through a portion of the domain of the United States until they secured passes, they were guiltless of infraction of any law, rule or order of their country, and were justified in their resistance.

The Arkansas company was composed of representative American citizens—prosperous men and women who were seeking homes in the "Golden West." And after being murdered under a flag of truce they were stripped of their clothing and left naked upon the desert, a prey to coyotes. Their property was divided among their assassins—an aggregation of religion crazed bandits whose only defense of their crime is the unsupported charge that the emigrants cursed the Mormons and boasted of having helped "kill old Joseph Smith."

As an illustration of the desperate and lying defense of the Mormon "prophets," and in defiance of the fact that Jacob Hamblin told him the whole truth of the massacre, Brigham Young, on January 6, 1858, wrote James W. Denver, commissioner of Indian affairs, Washington, D. C., as follows:

"Sir: On or about the middle of last September a company of emigrants traveling the southern route to California, poisoned the meat of an ox that died, and gave it to the Indians to eat, causing the immediate death of four of their tribe, and poisoning several others. This company also poisoned the water where they were encamped. This occurred at Corn creek, fifteen miles from Fillmore City. This conduct so enraged the Indians that they took measures for revenge."

The above letter from Brigham Young to James W. Denver has been herein proved to be totally and wickedly false, and as such, and as the best that the chief "prophet" could do to besmirch the memory of the emigrants, furnishes a complete vindication of the character of the Company that perished at the hands of Brigham Young's slaves at the Mountain Meadows on or about September 16, 1857.

And, in the final analysis, the reader should remember that Isaac C. Haight and others of the leading priesthood of the Parowan stake of Zion, some seven or eight days before the massacre, sent a message by James H. Haslam, to President Young inquiring as to the disposal of the emigrants. President Young's reply: "Permit the emigrants to go in peace," and his admonition to Haslam "not to spare horseflesh," so often and fervently quoted by Mormons, proves that President Young knew that the fate of the emigrants was at the disposal of the priesthood of the Parowan stake of Zion, and not at the disposal of the Indians. He had guilty knowledge that the massacre was contemplated by his slaves in Iron county. And although his farseeing statesmanship grasped the consequences of the deed, and although, when too late, and as a matter of policy, he did all that he could to stay the hands of his blood atoning assassins, he knew, when the massacre had been consummated, by whom the hellish deed had been done. Therefore, his letter to James W. Denver is proved to have been false in every respect, and that President Young descended to falsehood—even perjury—as a measure of protection for his people and his church.

ELDER PENROSE'S "DEFENSE" OF BRIGHAM YOUNG AND THE CHURCH.

On the evening of October 26, 1884, Elder Charles W. Penrose, then editor of the Deseret News, and since elevated to the apostolate, made a lengthy, rambling and mendacious address to a large audience of Saints in the twelfth ecclesiastical ward meeting house, Salt Lake City, and attempted to dispel the shadow that can never be lifted from the memory of those who, by their teachings and gross fanaticism, were responsible for the Mountain Meadows massacre. Penrose's was the first extended attempt to defend the Mormon "prophets," and it was a total failure.

In September, 1875, Brigham Young was summoned to appear as a witness in the first trial of John D. Lee. The condition of his health would not permit of his attendance, and in lieu thereof, certain interrogatories were forwarded to him at Salt Lake City, and which were answered by him under oath.

One question, only, and its answer are all that is required to prove that Brigham Young, or other affiants, testified falsely.

Question ninth—Did John D. Lee report to you at any time after this massacre what had been done at that massacre, and if so, what reply did you make to him in reference thereto?

Answer—Within some two or three months after the massacre he called at my office and had much to say with regard to the Indians, their being stirred up to anger and threatening the settlements of the whites, and then commenced giving an account of the massacre. I told him to stop, as from what I had already heard by rumor, I did not wish my feelings harrowed up with a recital of detail."

With seeming glee Elder Penrose quotes the above affidavit to prove that it was some time after the massacre before President Young knew anything about the affair further than "rumor," and that he would not permit Lee to tell the story. Then, with singular stupidity, Elder

Penrose proceeds to prove that President Young was a falsifier by putting his son's affidavit against that of his father's. Elder Penrose's hysterical zeal to also prove that Brigham Young did not know that the massacre had been concocted and perpetrated by the presiding priesthood of Iron county, led him into the fatal error of securing an affidavit from John W. Young to prove that Lee charged the massacre to the Indians. But that affidavit proved too much in another respect.

According to his affidavit, John W. Young, son of Brigham Young, was 13 years old at the time of the massacre, and was office boy for his father. After stating those facts Mr. Young continued as follows:

"I distinctly remember one day in the latter part of September, 1857, being in my father's office when John D. Lee, travel worn, entered the office and asked for a private interview with Governor Young.

"It is distinctly impressed on my mind beyond the power of time to efface, how Lee described the terrible deed which he said was committed by the Indians at Mountain Meadows."

From John W. Young's affidavit it is learned that Lee's visit was made immediately after the massacre, and that he did not "stop" at the command of President Young.

Not satisfied with pitting the affidavit of John W. Young against that of his father's, Elder Penrose secured a statement from Apostle Wilford Woodruff that, in every respect, supported the statements made by the "prophet's" son.

So eager was Elder Penrose to prove his stupidity and to fix the date of Lee's arrival at President Young's office, that he examined the voluminous diary kept by Apostle Woodruff and discovered that it was on September 29, 1857, or thirteen days after the tragedy at Mountain Meadows. No comment on the Woodruff and John W. Young contradictions to President Young's replies to the interrogatories in the Lee trial, and to his letter to James W. Denver, are necessary.

Elder Penrose's discourse in the twelfth ward was delivered more than seven years after the excution of Lee, and the world then knew a portion of the truth relative to the massacre. And in his anxiety to mitigate the hideousness of the crime, he committed the usual Mormon blunder of attacking the moral status of the murdered emigrants. If that were not his intent why did he quote the following paragraph from Apostle Woodruff's diary, and which had not the slightest bearing on the subject matter of his discourse?

"Brother Lee said he did not think there was a drop of innocent blood in the camp, for he had two of the children—(of the seventeen that were saved) in his house, and he could get but one to kneel down at prayer time, and the other would laugh at her for doing it, and they would swear like pirates.

(You elders of Israel will go into the canyons, and curse and swear, G—damn and curse your oxen, and swear by him who created you. I am telling you the truth. Yes, you rip and swear and curse as bad as any pirates ever did."

Doubtless Apostle Woodruff had, for the moment, forgotten the above selection from a sermon by Brigham Young in the early fifties Journal of Discourses, Vol. 1, page 211, and that "swearing like pirates" was not regarded as evidence that there "was not a drop of innocent blood" among the "elders of Israel"; and that profanity among the Saints in 1853 was not regarded as sufficient cause for blood atoning them. But the "elders of Israel" had entered into the "new and everlasting covenant," and were, therefore, immune from all crimes "except the shedding of innocent blood" or the blood of the Mormon "prophets.")

If the Indians, as alleged by John W. Young and Apostle Woodruff, had been the sole perpetrators of the crime, why the attempt to partially condone the crime of the redskins who knew absolutely nothing, and cared less, of the moral status of those whom they murdered? The more the "prophets" and their agents squirm and wriggle in their attempts to get from under the fearful responsibility for that crime the deeper do they sink into the quicksands of perfidy and guilt.

The massacre occurred on or about September 16, and John D. Lee was at President Young's office on the 29th. During the interim Lee remained a part of one day at the Meadows; it required one day for Lee to reach his home with the girls, and it would require full ten days to make the trip from Harmony to Salt Lake City. Therefore, the girls might, possibly, have been at Lee's residence two days before his departure for Salt Lake City. It was probably the second day after the massacre when Lee first asked the girls to join the family in prayers. Before those children, less than 8 years old, there was ever the vision of the slaughter. No doubt the girls had witnessed the murder of their mother, or mothers. Very likely they were clinging to their skirts when Lee and the others struck them down. Doubtless they had seen their older brothers and sisters slain by those monster fanatics of an alien church. Very likely they had heard McMurdy's frenzied cry of "O, Lord, my God, receive their spirits, it is for thy kingdom that I do this!" Is there wonder, then, that but one of those children knelt at prayer with the inhuman fanatic whose hands were red with the blood of their parents?

And those children "swore like pirates!" On the 16th of this month, September, 1910—the fifty-third anniversary of the massacre, while on a visit to the Mountain Meadows for the purpose of investigating the condition of the emigrants' grave, and to secure photographs of the grave and vicinity, the writer stood by the cairn on the desert. In imagination, the emigrants filed away up the valley under a flag of truce. Again the silence of that mountain solitude was broken by the cries of women, the screams of children and the rattle of firearms held by those wretched victims of blind obedience. Even after the lapse of fifty-three years, "swearing" would not only have been a relief, but would have been appropriate. Who, then, but arch-hypocrites could blame those girls for swearing? And who, but fiends incarnate, would claim that "there was not a drop of innocent blood in the camp" because one of those children refused to worship at the shrine of a god who would permit the representatives of his "holy prophets" to commit such a diabolical crime?

Apologists for, and defenders, by implication, of the Mountain Meadows massacre have ever attempted to palliate that crime by the besmirchment of the characters of the slain! Out upon such driveling, sickening cant and hypocrisy!

In defiance of the testimony of Jacob Hamblin during the second trial of Lee to the effect that "Pretty soon after it (the massacre) happened," he "told them (President Young and George A. Smith) everything I could," and his story was complete, Apostle Woodruff, in his affidavit, used by Elder Penrose, affirms that neither he nor Brigham Young knew anything about Lee's participation in the massacre until the year 1870, when they obtained the information from Apostle Erastus Snow of St. George, Utah! (It should be remembered that Jacob Hamblin's report was made to Brigham Young and George A. Smith.) Subsequently Lee was excommunicated in Salt Lake City, instead of in one of the southern stakes of Zion, where he could have secured witnesses, and have been "present in court." The haste and irregularity of Lee's excommunication prove that the belated act was forced by popular clamor—that it was merely an expedient, or grand stand play, with the express purpose of deceiving the people of the United States!

It may be contended by some of the "prophets" and their agents that the practice of blood atonement is a thing of the past. But, from the saints' viewpoint, it is a law of God, and his laws are eternal.

Given the absolute dominion for which these latter-day "prophets" are sleeplessly working, the torrid sermons of Brigham Young and

Jedediah M. Grant would be as mild in comparison as a summer zephyr to the vitriolic mouthings of the present insanely fanatical ruler of Joseph Smith's "Kingdom of God."

The hell born twins of unquestioning obedience and blood atonement are merely sleeping; the fires of Mormon fanaticism are merely smouldering. Yet, from the darkness of moral blindness and bigotry of Mormonism, the personality of Laban Morrill rises like a shaft of light, and serves notice to the world that there are Mormons who are infinitely better than their religion.

On a recent trip to the Meadows I went over to Pinto and from that point visited the scene of the massacre. It was my good fortune to be received at the home of Benjamin Platt, aged 78 years, who was working for John D. Lee at the time of the massacre. Mr. Platt is an intelligent Englishman, and withal a devout member of the Mormon church. It is to Mr. Platt that the public is indebted for the following information which was freely imparted during the ride over to the Meadows for the purpose of securing photographs of the "monument" and vicinity.

In the context of this story of the massacre Lee's version of the first attack by the Indians has been given, and in which Lee claims that he was not present. Mr. Platt avers that Lee's statement was not correct, and that the following version is the truth:

On the Sunday preceding the massacre fourteen Indians, an escort of the Cedar Lamanites, arrived at Lee's home at Harmony. Lee objected to accompanying the Indians, but after a brief consultation Lee departed with them toward the Meadows. Comanche, one of the reds, objected to the program of slaughter, but was finally induced to accompany the expedition.

Mr. Platt is relieved from responsibilty for the following narrative, but it is true, nevertheless. The party camped at Leachy spring. During the night the leader of the Indians dreamed that both his hands were filled with blood, and was alarmed at the significant omen. He related his dream, the next morning, to Lee who interpreted the "double handful of blood" as a victory for the redmen, and that they would secure the blood of the emigrants.

Mr. Platt's statement regarding the day of Lee's departure agrees with all the facts in the case, and which are as follows: The first attack took place at about daylight on Tuesday, and after which Lee went down to the Santa Clara river where, according to Lee's statement, he met Oscar Hamblin and fourteen other white men with a band of Indians. The second attack was made on Wednesday evening. On Thursday the militia arrived at the Meadows. The massacre was perpetrated on Friday. Early on Saturday morning Haight and Dame went from Hamblin's ranch over to the Meadows, and after viewing the results of the slaughter, and admonishing the elders to keep the fact of their participation a "secret forever," and to lay the burden of the crime on the Indians, the entire party left the Meadows for their homes. They could easily get to Leachy spring in time for the night's encampment, and Lee could easily reach his home early in the forenoon of Sunday, which is the day that Mr. Platt says he arrived in Harmony.

Mr. Platt related how Lee and his Indian escort rode into the stockade fort and around it to the well on the south side. In his autobiography Lee says that the Indians gave a whoop of victory, and after a repast on watermelons departed to their camp. Mr. Platt avers that the Indians made no oral demonstration of victory.

At the afternoon meeting of the Harmony Saints, according to Mr. Platt, John D. Lee gave a lurid description of the massacre, and that he seemed to glory in the deed which he said was the "will of the Lord." Asked if, in after years, Lee exhibited any feeling of remorse, Mr. Platt answered that he did not; that Lee was the same jovial, companionable man that he was prior to the massacre.

While condemning in the strongest and most earnest terms the leaders in the massacre, Mr. Platt averred that John D. Lee was the personification of hospitality toward all who called at Harmony, and related many acts of kindness and generosity to himself.

The years of silence on the massacre have passed, and the people of southern Utah now talk as freely of the tragedy as on any other subject, and deeply lament the ineffaceable stain that, unjustly, is the heritage of those who were residents of Iron and Washington counties at the time of the massacre, but who were guiltless of participation in, or sympathy with, the deed.

Many stories of the awful incidents, some true, others false, are in circulation among the people of southern Utah. Mr. Platt related a pitiful story about Albert, Hamblin's Indian boy, guarding the hiding place of the girls during several days, and secretly sharing his food, which he took over to the Meadows while herding cows in the vicinity, with Rachel and Ruth Dunlap before they were discovered, ravished and murdered as before related. But, unfortunately for the Indian boy, the story is not true.

Another interesting story, of the truth of which there is no doubt, was told by Mr. Platt as follows:

On one occasion when the emigrants were out of water they sent a child, a little girl dressed in white, to the spring. She was fired upon but escaped unharmed.

Notwithstanding that the people of southern Utah are familiar with nearly all the incidents of the massacre they have thus far, as a general truth, failed to grasp the central force that was responsible for the devilish act. Their abiding faith in the "divine mission of Joseph Smith," and their certainty that the Mormon "prophets" can do no wrong, blinds them to the forces that unerringly led up to the massacre. But there are scores of young men and women who are now demanding that the truth be told. Their reason teaches them that the assigned causes, or reasons, for the massacre, are insufficient to account for all the facts. They are now asking: "Why did those fifty-five men, professed followers of the merciful Son of God, commit a crime at which the civilized world stood aghast? If it was murder for plunder, why is it that only one assassin was punished for the crime when the name of every one of the murderers was known to the leading religious and civil authorities of Utah at the time of Lee's trial, or could have been obtained had there been any inclination to punish them? "There is something hidden," they say, "something mysterious and inexplicable as to the impelling motive to the crime. What is it?"

While not complete, the youth of Utah, and the people of the world, may, in the foregoing pages, learn the basic causes that led up to the Mountain Meadows massacre.

www.ingramcontent.com/pod-product-compliance
Lightning Source LLC
Chambersburg PA
CBHW080455170325
23595CB00010BA/1065